T0162646

A Journey into
Business

A Journey into
Business
Walk on the Wild Side

A practical guide to starting and
succeeding in business

KATE WILDE

authorHOUSE®

AuthorHouse™
1663 Liberty Drive
Bloomington, IN 47403
www.authorhouse.com
Phone: 1-800-839-8640

Published by AuthorHouse   09/11/2012

ISBN: 978-1-4772-2648-3 (sc)
ISBN: 978-1-4772-2649-0 (e)

Contents

Dedication

This book is for my daughter Verity, the light of my life.

ACKNOWLEDGEMENTS

This book could not have been written without the fabulous response I received when I first sent out e-mails asking for feedback from people I have had the pleasure and privilege to work with. With many of the replies I received a brief update on their business, so many success stories.

Some of these people are specifically mentioned in the book, they include Katrina Parsons, Trevor Starling, John Cator, Andrew Cropley, Paula Vika and others that I've not named but will know who they are. I would particularly like to thank Claire Wade, Martin Wright and Sally Porter for sharing their own business journeys with us, I hope that others will find inspiration in these case studies.

For bringing the book to life with the cover design I would like to thank Nick Applin and Nathan Ferguson of Ouch Creative Ltd.

Thinking about writing a book and actually doing it are two totally different things, but the person who gave me the confidence to write was Paul Hill who, as Business Editor for The Eastern Daily Press invited me to write a column for the newspaper. I think his exact words were "instead of bending my ear about all these things you have an opinion about, why don't you write a column?" Thank you Paul, this was my launch pad.

I would also like to thank Mike Barker, who has provided me with lots of material to write about and not forgetting Laura Kelly and Justine Dearden for their constant support, and for helping me when completion seemed so close, yet still so far.

Introduction

By watching many of the popular TV business programmes it is easy to believe that the business world is full of ruthless, aggressive people. Well that may be the case in the corporate world, but my world is small business, micro business, made up of decent hard working people who are passionate about what they do. They have a deep sense of integrity and although they are in business to make money, that is rarely the driving force. As confidence is gained many people find success brings them financial rewards beyond all they dared imagine. Welcome to the world of the self-employed, small business owner.

Having spent the last 12 years training, advising and mentoring people who have taken the big brave step into self-employment I found that every now and again someone will come up to me and say "I always remember what you told me about . . . . and I still use your advice." For whatever reason, the words have stayed with them, some business tip which has become imbedded in their minds and in many cases used to great effect. I realised that if I could collect all these golden nuggets of information together I could use them as the basis for a book, a practical, useful book to help other people who were just starting out in business.

I had toyed with the idea of writing for many years and although I recognised that I could use it as a means of sharing my knowledge and experience, producing yet another guide to success in business wasn't enough. I also felt that there was a big gap in the market because most of the books available seem to be aimed at 'entrepreneurs' the real trail blazers, but the majority of people don't see themselves in this way, they are simply self-employed.

Following my initial plea for help the feedback began to follow. I was quite amazed at some of the things that had been remembered, often throw away comments from me but somehow they resonated with the people that have attended my workshops.

I decided that by collecting these anecdotes and stories I could offer a book full of really useful tips. My hope is that those who read this book will identify with, and use the experience of others to help them along the path of business success.

I too have been inspired by many gifted speakers and authors. There is no copyright on their wise words or on anything that I have to say, it is all to be shared. It is my hope that what I have written does get shared and is used to good effect and to help those that want to start, grow and succeed in business.

The Ingredients of Success

Self-employment doesn't suit everyone, for many people the thought of running their own business is a dream come true bringing independence, flexibility and control of their life. But many people need the structure that employment brings, the routines, operating under instruction and regular pay. Of course if you've only ever known life as an employee you won't know if self-employment suits you until you start working for yourself. It's all a bit of a gamble, but let's see how well you measure up against our checklist of attributes generally associated with people who run successful businesses.

Checklist for the Ingredients of Business Success.

1. **Attitude**—the reality is that you can have a great business idea, the perfect plan, funding in place and still fail. Alternatively you can have a half baked idea, ride by the seat of your pants and make a fortune. It all comes down to having the right attitude. If your attitude is poor, your chances of succeeding are seriously limited. There are many characteristics that are recognised as common amongst those who do succeed, you may have to work at developing some of them, but with the right attitude, anything is possible.

2. **Self-confidence**—so many people lack self-confidence and this is often the reason for not getting the business off the ground at all. Are some people born with confidence and others none? Or is it a combination of experience, attitude and positivity that gives us confidence?

3. **Self-belief**—if you don't believe in yourself and your ability to make the business work, why should anyone else? Other people can often create the problem for you, by passing on their own lack self-belief, ignore them, and learn to believe that things are possible. Focus on the person you want to become.

4. **Self-motivation**—it can be hard to remain motivated especially when negatives are being thrown at you but you have to learn to pick yourself up and stay focussed. Try to get into the habit of reminding yourself of past successes, what you are good at and current advantages and opportunities which lay ahead.

5. **Self-discipline**—willpower, restraint, these need to be exercised continuously. Self discipline can be the difference between someone with average ability achieving something amazing as opposed to someone with an exceptional talent never realising their potential. Self discipline is like a muscle, it can be developed.

6. **Good communication skills**—we communicate on many levels—written, oral, and of course through body language. It's good to remember that communication is a two way process and there is a good reason why we have two ears and one mouth, remember to use them in that order. *'Effective communication is not a science to be learnt, it is an art to be practiced.'*

7. **Assertiveness**—firm and slightly forceful but definitely in control. Assertiveness is about being able to make a confident statement that affirms your rights or points of view. This should be done without aggressively threatening or assuming dominance or submissively allowing another to ignore you or your points of view.

8. **Resilient**—I remember reading a Chinese proverb which says that a successful person is one who gets knocked down 7 times but gets up 8 times. Your level of resilience will determine whether you succeed or fail.

9. **Focussed**—be clear about what it is you want and go for it. Having clearly defined goals and knowing where you are heading helps. Break these down into bite sized pieces so that you can see that they are achievable.

10. **Ability to use the whole of your brain**—we often hear about left or right brain 'types' of people but to successfully run a business you must be able to use the whole of your brain, to be organised, analytical and creative.

"One thing that sticks in my mind is when I told you that I had bought 10,000 envelopes. Your response was that you were not impressed that I had bought 10,000 envelopes but you knew I was determined to fill them with my handmade wedding stationery (and presumably not just fill them but sell them). I think this showed something of my determination, Self-belief, and Self-confidence." John

John had many of the ingredients necessary for the success he enjoys. Although he has a naturally creative mind, the more analytical side had worked out that if he was to earn money from making cards and wedding stationery he had to have a production line approach to his work, to create volume. Filling 10,000 envelopes was his first goal.

How well did you score?

10 /10 would be ideal but as I have said already if your attitude is right and you recognise your own, and often self-imposed limitations and work on them, why shouldn't you be successful?

Are you ready to continue?

Key Learning Point

Self-employment is not for everyone but if you think you have what it takes, get ready to take that leap.

The Next Step

To actually take that leap of faith is a really big moment. There are no guarantees, and no matter how much market research you carry out this can only give you information on the past and the present. Your business success is in the future.

"If you don't give it a go, are you going to look back in 20 years time and wish you had?"

I remember saying these exact words to Katrina. Her passion and her business is to help people learn to cook good basic family food instead of opening jars and packets or resorting to convenience food. I knew that if she didn't give it a chance she would probably regret missing the opportunity for the rest of her life.

There are lots of reasons why you may decide to start a business. Whatever the reason, the business you chose will almost certainly be something you enjoy, are very good at or you have identified a great opportunity or a niche market. Many people are attracted by the independence that self-employment offers, not having to ask permission or refer to your line manager for a decision. For others it is the flexibility that it offers, work the hours that you want to, take Thursday afternoon off but start at 5.30 a.m. the following morning, whatever it takes, the choice is yours.

There is a down side of course. Along with your independence comes total responsibility, you make all the decisions, you don't have anyone to refer to or to get advice from and sometimes you will get it wrong.

Getting things wrong is all part of learning, but whenever you can, watch and learn from the mistakes of others.

If you have worked as an employee in a large organisation for many years the adjustment can be quite a challenge. Realising that there is no one to bounce ideas around with, no one to say 'well done' or review your work with you can take some getting used to. For those who choose to work on a self-employed basis especially if you are based at home the biggest challenge is often the loneliness and isolation. Even if you start off with an abundance of confidence and self-belief, if you spend too many hours alone you can lose some of your drive. Think about your day and how you can gain some interactivity with real people.

"If you don't have a dog, get one. Take it for walks several times a day because it is a great way to meet people including potential customers."

This little gem came about because I had several people attending my workshops who had been recommended by Gary, a guy they had met while walking their dogs. I knew exactly who they meant and I wouldn't be surprised if Gary didn't even have a dog. He is someone who would happily walk along with a lead if he had some slow time, whistling to a dog in hiding. Gary runs a very successful business and rarely misses an opportunity to network and to sell.

Just because you are working from home and can wear anything you like it doesn't mean that you need to get sloppy. Why not adopt a uniform of some kind, or dress for business. Not only does this help you get into the right mindset but gives a clear message to others that you are unavailable. Friends that know you are at home and drop in for a coffee will get the message or in the case of your family, they will know that you are unable to attend to their immediate needs.

"One of the things I am becoming more aware of is how focussed I need to be now that I am working from home. I remember that you told me about someone actually leaving the house and coming back in again to give them the right mindset to start work. I'm thinking of trying this."

"I took your advice and now my aging mother knows that if I am wearing my tabard I am working and not available to make her a cup of tea and sit down for a chat."

In the early stages it is often tempting to try to keep a foot in both camps of self-employment and employment. Trying to please an employer and dedicate time to getting a new business off the ground is very challenging although often necessary for financial reasons. It's not usually too long before something has to give. The result will be that you either give up on the business idea because you are unable to commit the amount of time needed and therefore lose focus, or you will walk away from the employed work and give your business full throttle.

"You stressed that the mindset for employed and self-employed are quite different and it is difficult to get a business off the ground while remaining employed. You didn't say it was impossible but without giving 100% to a new business, you are much less likely to succeed. I am about to quit the day job and go for it, the time is right."

Key Learning Point

The success of your business depends upon you. Get into the right mindset and make it happen.

So you think you have a Great Idea for a Business?

Having a great idea for a business is one thing but before launching full steam ahead it makes sense to have some evidence to support this, find out if other people think your idea is good too. People often think they need in depth analysis with lots of tables and charts, sector reports, customer demographics etc. In some cases this might be necessary but generally there are some basic common sense questions that we need to find the answers to.

By carrying out market research we provide evidence that our business idea is viable; there are things that we need to know rather than taking a guess at, making assumptions is a dangerous thing to do. We need to understand the market place, and our customers.

It is usual to begin testing your ideas with family and friends, but be warned.

"Be cautious when you ask the opinions of family and friends as they can be biased and they will usually tell you what they think you want to hear. Always seek independent, constructive advice."

Alternatively, your family and friends may feel the need to protect you from disappointment, usually because *they* can't see how the business will work. More to the point, they can't see or believe that they could make it work and if they can't, surely you can't either? Recognise that these are their self-limiting beliefs.

The internet and use of search engines has made a huge difference to the way in which we are able to carry out research. In the past it would have taken months if not years to collect, in fact it's hard to imagine life without Google. In addition to desk research it is also important to carry out some field research—talk to people, surveys, questionnaires, interviews, observations and test marketing are important too.

Based on the information that you collect you can see patterns forming, you will identify trends and begin to collect statistics which will help you to make predictions about the future. Although we can make sensible and often pretty accurate predictions this research is based on historical information which comes with no guarantees for the future. It is still down to you to make it all happen.

Your research is important. A business that understands the market, its customers and competitors and uses this information effectively will sell more.

You Need to Know:

Who will your target customers be?

"I now realise how important it is to know who you are targeting. What does your typical customer look like—age, gender etc. what are their habits, what do they read, and what other products do they buy? How can we encourage them to change their buying habits and buy from us?"

You need to be clear about your target market, know who it is you are planning to sell to so that any advertising or promotional activity you carry out hits that target. You can then be sure that you are using language which is understood by your potential clients and that they are receptive to it. For example if we know that our target market is professional women aged between 40-60 the language you use will be quite different to that which we would use to sell to a teenage market.

It may be that you want to sell a wide range of products to all ages, male and female. This may be the case but if you try to get a message across that is totally inclusive you will most likely dilute it to the point that nobody is really sure about what you are offering or to whom. Work out which section of the market is going to bring in the best returns and focus on them first.

USP (Unique Selling Point)

What is so special about what you have to offer? What is your unique selling point—USP?

You need to give your customers a good reason to choose you to buy from. Unless you have a new product there is every chance that your potential customer already has a supplier, so why should they change and buy from you? It could be that you are the best at what you do, because of the excellent customer service you offer, the range of products, or the design of the packaging. The one thing you don't want to aim for is to be the cheapest. There is only ever one company that is the cheapest and by competing to be cheaper you won't make any money. You need to charge enough to enable you to do your job properly, to give added value wherever possible and to build customer loyalty. People who always buy the cheapest generally have no loyalty.

Market Position

"You told me to decide where I want to position my business in the market; am I a John Lewis or a Primark store? I took a deep breath and decided to go for top end customers and now everything that I do reflects this with my quality products and excellent customer service."

Consistency in your approach is what is needed. As customers, if we go into a top end store we have an expectation that anything we buy will be a quality item and therefore probably expensive. We will select from a display, expect to be served by a trained and informed member of staff and items will be wrapped and placed in a quality carrier bag. If we have a problem with our purchase we know that by returning the items our complaints will be dealt with and a solution found.

Alternatively if we buy from the low end of the market we accept that we get what we pay for if it all falls apart—well that's not a surprise and there is probably no point in taking it back as the replacement will fall apart just as quickly, because it was cheap.

Choose your market position and stick to it, be consistent at all times.

How Much Do I Charge?

Often there is a going rate for many products and services, you can stick with this average price or you can bring in some of the considerations we have just mentioned—market position, your USP or the added value you will offer. Many people who are new to business under value themselves quite considerably and through a lack of self-confidence will sell far too cheaply because they are new.

"When I first started my business I decided to price myself cheaper than my competitors because they had more experience than me. You told me to start with a higher price but offer discounts for the first few months rather than be seen to put the prices up once I'd found my feet. This worked for me and I now feel confident to charge the standard rate and more with some add on sales."

Who are my competitors?

You need to know everything there is to know about who you are competing against. Who are their target customers? How and where do they promote their business? How much do they charge? What is their USP? What do they do well? What do they not do well?

It's a good idea to draw up a chart and list your competition with answers to the above questions to give you a clear understanding of what the real head on competition is and how crowded the market place is, or isn't.

Key Learning Point

Carry out your market research and do not ignore findings which contradict your preconceptions.

CASE STUDY

Sally Porter—Decorate Your Cake

Sally first began thinking about starting her own business at least eighteen months before taking any action, but the desire to do something for herself was ever present and growing and suddenly it felt that the time was right. Sally had always loved decorating cakes and was working part time selling cake decoration products while her children were young but she was bored with this and needed a challenge.

"I signed up for a business start-up workshop and after that there was no going back. I felt totally inspired and motivated to get started and although I had planned to keep my part time job for a while I gave notice immediately, I knew what I wanted to do and there was no turning back.

I soon discovered that I had entered a whole new world. Marketing, paperwork, establishing new contacts, endless e-mails, everything seems to hit you at once. I wanted everything in place straight away but it doesn't work like that, designing websites and business stationery takes time. While all of this was happening I wasn't earning money but it knew it was important for me to stay focussed.

I joined networking groups and found that by meeting with the same people on a regular basis a deep sense of trust and support develops. More recently I have developed new circles of contacts by becoming involved with different groups, as I grow I find my needs are changing.

Although I was enjoying myself creating beautiful cake decorations I soon discovered that there was very little money to be made in this highly competitive market, the amount of money going out was much higher than expected with many hidden costs. I also realised that I was spending a lot of time baking cakes when what I really wanted to do was to decorate them.

I needed to make changes and so I took time to think about what I really wanted to achieve, I decided to focus on cake craft workshops, demonstrations and corporate team building events. I enjoy this so much more and there is no shortage of people who want to learn cake decorating skills and have some fun at the same time.

Three years into the business I now have a very clear vision for the future. Within five years I will have my own premises for creative workshops; these will be supported by on-line sales of all things creative in baking.

Having the support of my family has been important. They are now used to not having a meal on the table at six and know that just because I am at home I am working and not readily available to them. My husband helps me with the paperwork which I really do not enjoy doing myself and my sons have become more responsible and offer me continuous encouragement and support. They keep me on track if things are not going well.

I recognise that I have changed over the past three years, other people see this too. My self-confidence has grown, there was a time when I was terrified at the thought of public speaking but I have no problem with this now the scariness has gone.

I am doing what I enjoy and when I look back and realise how far I have come I get a wonderful feeling of satisfaction."

Business Planning

Business planning is often thought about in the context of raising finance and having something to show to the bank or whoever the lenders may be. In reality the most important reason for writing a business plan is for yourself to help you define your ideas and focus your mind. But where do you start?

The most important element of the business plan is your vision for the future, your destination in this business journey and the goals that you set yourself which will help take you closer to achieving your vision. Be brave, sit back and close your eyes, think ahead to the future. What do you see?

Starting a new business is a journey and there are many analogies I could use but my favourite is to imagine setting off for a walk through the woods. Often you find in public woodland there are paths marked out for you, follow the red circle for a two mile walk, blue triangle for five miles and a yellow square for a ten mile hike. As long as you follow the path you have chosen you will reach your destination. You may decide to take a look over a hill, a little off track, this is OK, you won't get lost if you keep an eye on the path marked out, you can always find your way back to it. It may be that you like what you see over the hill, if you follow a new path it will take you in a completely new direction, you have a choice, but the path that was marked out will still be there for you to go back to.

This is how a business plan can work for you. It maps out your path, allows you to look at new opportunities, accepts that things do change sometimes, but is there for you to go back to when you are ready, to remind you of your chosen destination, your ultimate goal.

It may be that in the early stages all you can focus on is your first paying customer, at some point you need to move beyond this. Give some thought to your own progression needs, the chances are you will want to grow the business, diversify in some way or move onto something new. It's unlikely that you will stand still for too long.

Many people start off in business without planning, jumping straight in, they have an idea, and are off. They learn as they go along and quite often it all falls into place and they find they have a successful business. Or it may just look like this on the surface and their success comes from their determination and drive. They don't dwell on the mistakes they make, (many of them costly in terms of time and money) they learn from their mistakes and move on, but only they need to know that. Think how much more successful they may have been if they had taken the time to think things through and had formed a plan.

"My dad has been in business for the past thirty years and he says he has made just about every mistake possible and it has cost him a fortune. He has never had a plan, he has just learnt the hard way."

Other people recognise the value in gathering as much information as they can and whether they approach it formally or informally will begin to put together their plan. We hear the words business plan all the time but what is a business plan, what does it look like, can you do it yourself or do you need an accountant to help you? You would think that the solution would be easily available on the internet but trying to find an example of one that you can relate to is not that simple and the whole process can look quite daunting.

"One piece of advice that springs to mind is how you installed into me the importance of planning, this has been vital to us in every aspect of our business."

The reality is that many people don't write their thoughts and ideas down but they do plan, often just in their head. Now while this may work for some people it's unlikely that this kind of planning will cover everything and some important details can easily be missed out. There is a great deal of evidence to show that by writing your thoughts and ideas down and making sure that there is continuity, you will become far more focussed. It will give you a check list to make sure you have considered all that is relevant to the development of your idea. You are much more likely to achieve your goals and waste less time and money than if you don't plan.

Writing Your Business Plan

Where do you start? The first step might be to talk your ideas through, preferably with someone outside your circle of family and friends. Once you have said the words it suddenly becomes a little more real.

"When I first said my idea out loud all my thoughts like 'is it a silly idea, can I really do that?' simply disappeared. Talking it through with strangers gave me the confidence and also the commitment to make it happen."

Writing a business plan is not rocket science. Like most things in business, it is plain common sense. It is about putting down your thoughts of how you are going to conduct business in a logical order. If you are planning a micro business the completed document is likely to be about 12 pages including financial information. If you are employing staff and taking on premises there will be more to it. If you have carried out a lot of market research which needs to be included this is usually placed at the back of the document as appendices with reference made to it in your text, rather than the main body of the plan.

"When you first talked to me about business plans I didn't think I would need one because I didn't want to borrow any money. In reality I found the thought of writing it all down quite daunting. I'm so glad I did write one, it was such a worthwhile exercise. I am much more focussed now and because I can see on paper how it works I can really believe in it and move forward with confidence."

There are dozens of templates to help you write your plan, some can look quite scary particularly when it comes to the cash flow and profit/ loss forecasting. Others are so basic that they don't challenge your thoughts or encourage you to think them through in sufficient depth. Often a combination of one or two different templates will be the answer and these can come from banks who will usually provide you with an information pack full of useful information, or from one of many websites including my own www.engagewithbusiness.co.uk.

A good approach when trying to work out what to include in your business plan is to turn things on their head, a trick I often find useful. Imagine you have some funds that you would like to invest in a business, what would you want to know about the business idea to help you decide if it is a worthwhile investment of your money?

The key points to consider are—

- What are they planning to do, what are the business aims, goals, visions for the future?

- What service or products are they offering, the business model and some rational behind their thinking.

- Who is involved and what skills and experience do they have?

- What evidence is there to suggest the idea is viable? Market research.

- How are they going to make it happen? Their marketing and sales strategy.

- How will it be paid for? Capital funding, sales, cash flow and profit /loss forecasts.

These are the foundations upon which to build, there is of course much more to think about but this will get you started.

If you find that things are just not quite hanging together as you think they should, take a step back, look at it from a different angle, work out which part of it you are not comfortable with. It may be that you need to consider a different approach or a new way of looking at things. Are you perhaps moving away from your core principles?

When you decide that the time has come to write the plan don't expect to sit down and write it in a couple of hours and then put it aside as the job done. The plan will evolve over time and may need to constantly be tweaked and updated. One thing that should remain consistent is your vision, what you are aiming for in the future. It may be that you've not thought about anything more than getting your first customer, but take time to think about this because some of the decisions you need to make now may be influenced by where you want to be in ten years time.

Different people find different ways of preparing a business plan. What works for me is to start with a mind map and I use a white board or flip chart because I find this less restrictive to my thought process and the need to express them. The mind map helps me to explore opportunities and develop new ideas.

The next step is to put things into a logical order of headings and perhaps begin to add some bullet points under each heading. From here I begin to write the more formal business plan with full text beneath each heading with reference to any additional information I may have included in the appendices.

Sales, cash flow, and profit/loss forecasts. This financial information is what will hold the plan together. The idea is that you go through every part of the business plan and identify where you have stated an action that requires funding. Be sure to include everything and allow for sundry items you don't yet know you need. The sales forecast figures will come from your marketing plan. If you have really thought through how you are going to make sales the numbers will be easier to forecast. I usually find that people need to rethink their commitment to marketing at this stage.

Present your figures on spread sheets with a paragraph explaining to the reader what they are looking at.

Use of language and whether it should be written in the first or third person are questions which often crop up. I think that if it is a micro business, where essentially the business is you, you should write in the first person using 'I', 'me'. If the business includes a number of people, is incorporated (Ltd.) you should use third person reference.

The next step is to find someone to read the plan who does not know about you or your ideas for a business. Invite them to critique and challenge some of what you have written.

There does however come a point in time when you have to stop planning and actually do something if your business idea is ever going to get off the ground.

We have begun to uncover the mystery of the business plan. By reading the rest of this book you will begin to build a picture in your own mind of how your business will shape up. Keep a note book handy and learn from what others have to say, people who have been right where you are now, at the start of this exciting journey into business.

Key Learning Point

Writing a business plan will help you to think your ideas through and gain focus.

GETTING YOUR BUSINESS STARTED

Timing is important but usually if you have taken the idea this far all you need is a leap of faith.

"Stop planning and start doing—this really inspired me to get off my backside and find some customers. As a result I plucked up the courage to set up a meeting with a local theme park. I won the contract to supply them with quiches and started delivering to them the week after my training with you. Feeling inspired, I contacted local farm shops, which resulted in contracts to supply quiches, pies and sausage rolls all within 3 weeks of training. I had enough new customers within three weeks of your training to start trading!"

So let's put the writing of the business plan aside for now and start thinking about how to get this business moving.

Knowing what you want to achieve and developing your ideas to turn this into a reality is a good place to start, your vision for the future. It can seem like an impossible dream but if you were standing at the foot of a mountain about to start a climb you would probably feel the same way. The peak of the mountain is so high how will you ever reach it? That is until you realise that climbing a mountain is a staged journey with stops along the way. You will set out with a map and compass and enough supplies for the journey. There are places where you will rest, set up base camp, test and measure the environment and keep going until you get to the top.

Planning to start a business, having a vision and setting goals is a journey. Make sure you have a plan, (your map) the right equipment, enough supplies, and away you go.

"You said that I shouldn't be afraid to follow where the opportunities are taking me, it may not be in the direction I had originally planned but go with it, check it out. This is certainly the case for me with new opportunities unfolding that I would never have considered when I first started."

You really do have to keep an open mind when you start a business because the biggest problem is that 'you don't know what you don't know'. This does present you with a problem, how can you plan what you don't know for goodness sake? Hopefully the one thing that will remain consistent is your vision for the future. Where do you want to be in five or ten year's time? Some people may have more ambition than others; you may plan to develop a national brand, to franchise, to grow a business to pass down to your children, overseas trade and global domination. Others may just want to tick over and create a perfect work/life balance for themselves and their family.

Key Learning Point

Is the time right? Just do it.

Vision, Mission and Goal Setting

Many people dream of having their own business and just a few turn that dream into a reality. There is a big difference between having a dream and a vision, a vision is when you can begin to see how everything will fit into place, step by step, until at some time in the future it becomes a reality.

Vision/Mission Statement

You may think that having a 'vision statement' or 'mission statement' may seem like something that belongs in the corporate world with some marketer coming up with a few lines of rhetoric and a strap line, but it has its place with small businesses too.

Businesses, large or small, that are run by leaders with a clear vision, a vision which is shared throughout the organisation are likely to be far more successful.

The difference between a vision and a mission statement is that the vision statement focuses on the big picture—what you or the organisation wants to become. The mission statement is how this vision will be implemented.

In the corporate world it may seem empty and meaningless but for a small business it can serve you very well. It can underpin your values, the culture of your business, and your promise to your customers. A strap line can summarise the vision/mission nicely and can be an effective addition to your marketing tool kit.

Not everyone has hugely ambitious plans, while some strive for global domination others are happy to just earn a living and strike a work/life balance. It is not unusual to find that after trading for a while, and your self-confidence has grown, ideas that have stayed at the back of your mind start working their way forward. Suddenly it doesn't seem like the impossible dream, ambition kicks in.

There are a number of things that you may want to think through at an early stage, sooner rather than later, things that may have an impact on the longer term. For example, you may want to develop your business into a nationally recognised brand perhaps with a view of franchising. If this is the case having a well-designed logo from the start that sits proudly alongside national brand logos is sensible. Choosing a name for your business, the legal status, even an exit strategy are all things that should be considered with a view of where you are heading in the future.

We are all different in how we see things, some of us have special moments, often at the start of the day when everything suddenly seems so clear and we know exactly what to do, it almost feels like a gift. Others choose their destination, they focus entirely on what they want to achieve and work relentlessly towards achievement.

Visualise Success

Use visualisation, see success, know what it looks like. Have pictures on your wall of the type of house you want to live in, the car you want to drive and the lifestyle you want to lead. Run your own movie trailer in your head where amazing things are happening with you at the centre of it all.

Write your goals down and make sure they are specific. Please don't write things like—in five years the business will be established. Do write something along the lines of in five years we will have a turnover of £150,000, profit of £80,000 a database of 150 regular customers and be sufficiently busy to employ staff. Putting measures in place will help you to know when you are achieving your goals. If you are exceeding them maybe you set them too low or you are doing better than you ever imagined possible. Please be realistic.

Turnover and profit are easy ways to measure progress but for many people it's not about the money. Success means different things to different people and maybe the focus is on your work/life balance, spending quality time with your family. They have to be your goals.

Monitor your progress and set indicators to measure your success. If you are not close to achieving your goals after the first year you will have a chance to re-evaluate the amount of time and effort you are putting into the business and into your marketing strategy.

Are you following the right path?

There have been times through discussion about business ambitions, I find I'm not convinced that the person talking to me whole heartedly believes in the goals they have set themselves. Often this is because there is an ingredient missing, things are not coming together, not feeling right and often it requires simple adjustments.

"You suggested that I stick to what I know best, which is the 5* hospitality design industry. I am so glad that I did, I have re-established old contacts and am about to fly off to Hong Kong to complete a deal. I am so much more comfortable with this market that I know so well as opposed to residential design which is where I thought I was heading."

Key Learning Point

If you don't know where you're going, all roads lead there.
—Roman Proverb

YOU AND WHO ELSE?

It's really useful to take time to analyse the skills that you have for business, in particular to recognise what you are really good at. This includes a range of natural attributes, together with skills learnt through attending workshops or formal training and transferable skills from other life experiences. Don't ever under estimate the value of some of the skills that you developed from what may seem totally unrelated experiences. Women/mothers in particular develop excellent organisation and communication skills, rounding up children and gently persuading them to wear this, go there, and eat this you will enjoy it. These transferable skills do have a place in business. Being able to communicate effectively to ensure that a five year old understands and co-operates is indeed a skill. If you can communicate effectively to a five year old you are more likely to get a clear message across to an adult.

Consider the gap between the skills that you have and the range of skills that will be useful. Identify areas where you need to get some training or where you will need to buy in some expertise.

Even though you may be a sole trader with no intention of ever employing staff there will be times when you will need to use the skills and expertise of professionals. Most new business owners have a limited budget and so have to do most things themselves; there may not be a choice, plan wisely before spending so that you get the best possible return on your investment.

The Accountant

For many people finding and appointing an accountant is a declaration that you are in business, after all, meeting with an accountant is what business people do. Many owners of small businesses manage without an accountant. They keep simple accounts which they are quite capable of submitting via the internet (filing on line) for themselves and therefore saving money.

It is so often said that any good accountant will save you more in taxes than the cost of their services and to some extent this is true if your turnover is sufficient to find the savings. Finding the right accountant to meet the needs of your business is not always easy. There are different levels of skill and accreditation which will reflect in what you get for your money.

Let's start with the book keeper. They will be able to organise your income and expenditure invoices and record this information in a format that suits you which could be paper based, computer spreadsheets or using accounting software. They may be able to complete and file your tax return too.

The next level is someone who will keep records for you as above, file your tax return, and offer some advice about tax efficiency and allowances that you may be entitled to claim. One of the main benefits here is that you will feel the assurance that everything which is needed for compliance purposes is covered.

The next level is the larger accountancy firm, usually with partners who have a wide range of expertise to share with you, but at a cost.

"When I first started out I used an accountant who was recommended by a friend, they were good value for money, and I had the reassurance

that everything that the tax man needed was covered. But as the business began to grow I realised that I had outgrown my accountant. I now needed advice on the best ways to finance business growth in a tax efficient way, to understand any pitfalls and to feel that there was real financial control within my business. I had a chat with a partner in one of the big local firms and straight away I recognised the value he could bring and although I don't look forward to receiving his invoice I feel the investment is good value for money."

If you have plans for business growth it is as well to find an accountant with the expertise to support your ambition from an early stage.

It's worth mentioning at this point that there is a big difference between keeping records for compliance purposes e.g. keeping the tax man happy and having financial information available for decision making purposes. To ensure that you maintain financial control of your business you need to have access to up to date information which will help you make informed business decisions. You must also remember that although you may take advice from a professional, complying with tax regulations is your responsibility. Be sufficiently informed, don't just hand it over to someone else, financial control and financial management are the key to business success.

The Solicitor

Solicitors can seem to be very expensive but so can not taking good legal advice. Many templates and guides are available to save you time in front of a solicitor while the clock is ticking, but having the professional eye cast over your contracts to add some legal spin can save you a fortune at a later date. A perfect example of good legal advice saving money is with drawing up partnership or shareholder agreements, more about this later.

Many solicitors will offer the first thirty minutes free of charge giving you the opportunity to decide if you feel you can work with them, so give them an interview.

"I was half way through the planning stages of preparing to film a short video for a client. I had put in a good many hours planning the locations, arranging to hire specific audio equipment when they changed their mind about going ahead. They thought they could just cancel my service and not pay for the time I had already spent on the project service. I realised that if I had proper terms and conditions drawn up and signed at the outset I could have avoided what then turned into a very difficult situation. The cost of using a solicitor to write an agreement specific to my needs was far less than the amount I stand to lose with customers cancelling in this way."

The Graphic Designer

So much will depend upon the type of business you are planning but in most cases some investment in good design and branding is money well spent. Having a professional brand identity can have a huge impact on the public perception, in particular the thoughts your customers will have of you and your business. Even if a friend or family member is a talented artist and able to design a logo this is not the same as having a professional produce something that has commercial appeal. It is quite easy to see who has invested in their brand identity and those who have not. Not investing in your branding also says a lot about you and your business.

"I found some free designs on the internet and managed to produce some business cards and leaflets which I thought were OK, they represented me and what I had to offer, and they were cheap. After hearing what you had to say about the power of the brand I decided to get a professional to advise me. These guys took my original design to a whole new level. The colours

are the same and it still has the gentle feel that I was keen to capture but now it looks so professional, it has put me in a whole new league. With my new image I have received such a confidence boost I have increased my prices by 25% and I am attracting new customers each week and business is growing. I feel like a professional and my customers now see me as a professional too."

Whenever you are choosing a professional to work with it is wise to go by recommendation, look at examples of their work and decide for yourself if you feel comfortable working with them. After all they are about to become part of your team. Where design is concerned be sure that the ownership of the design is transferred to you.

The Web Designer

Choosing a web designer is similar in many ways to choosing a graphic designer, use someone who had been recommended, has produced designs that you like and that you feel you can work with. Web design can be carried out remotely, you may never need to see the designer but unless you know exactly what you want and can give very specific instructions via e-mail I recommend that you choose someone that you are comfortable to sit and chat with, someone who has the ability to draw your ideas out and using skill and experience, develop a website that works for you.

When it comes to planning your website there are a few things to think about in advance. What purpose does it serve? Is it to inform, an on-line brochure showing current projects or past work or do you want to sell from it? Choosing and registering domain names, hosting, setting up e-mail accounts are all things that a web designer can do for you but be careful about how much control you give them. Check out any hidden costs for hosting, system updates and support.

Many web designers offer Content Managed Systems (CMS). With a few lessons and some initial back up support you will be able to manage the site quite nicely yourself. Uploading photos and videos, updating text can all be done very easily with most CMS systems. This is highly preferential to waiting for your designer to attend to it and it won't be a priority compared with other work of higher financial value. From the designers point of view handing over responsibility for updates to clients is a far more cost effective way of working.

Making sure that a website is regularly updated and is fully optimised with the search engines (SEO, Search Engine Optimisation) is time demanding so you will need to invest your time into this or pay someone to do it for you. Having a website is one thing, being found on the World Wide Web is another.

Mentors and Advisers

Having a mentor or business adviser is highly valuable to anyone starting out in business. They are there to be used as a soundboard, to test your ideas, to support your decision making and to challenge you at times. And why stop at one? Why only one mentor, have more so that you have different skill sets to draw upon? To contradict myself in the same paragraph, beware of too much conflicting advice and opinions which can sometimes cloud your judgement.

There are, and will undoubtedly, continue to be various schemes that recruit voluntary mentors with a view of matching them with entrepreneur mentees. While this can work out really well it depends entirely upon the luck of the draw as to who you are matched with.

Some of my most rewarding work has been through voluntary mentoring working with The Princes Trust. My mentee was really hard work to start with, she spoke very little English, had arrived in the UK a couple of years before as a refugee. Today she is a UK citizen, home owner and a business owner. We lost contact for a while but last year she phoned me to say that she was a finalist in a national hairdressing competition. She told me this:

"Although I always valued your support I don't think I realised just how important it was for me to have a mentor. When I stood in line with the other hairdressers at the competition I realised something. I realised that they were mostly men and women with scissors, but you made me a business woman, and I want to thank you for that."

Partnerships

I am always wary of partnerships.

"I hate to admit you were right but we had been friends for over 20 years and after six weeks in business together we are not even speaking to each other. I can't say you didn't try to warn us."

This news made me feel very sad but it was predictable. When I first met the two ladies I challenged them about why they wanted to work as a partnership but they were adamant that they had been friends for such a long time and wanted to work together and this is what they were going to do.

The reality was that one of them had a fairly good understanding of business and had recently been made redundant, the other was unhappy with her current employer. While one of them began to set up the business and find potential clients the other clearly just wanted to be employed. Unfortunately she also thought that self-employment meant that she only had to work when she wanted and on her terms, regardless of the needs of the clients or her business partner. How wrong can anyone be?

If someone approaches you with an invitation to set up a partnership ask yourself why they are not setting up alone, why do they need you? It may be that they are looking for a balance of skills or they may need propping up because they don't have the confidence or capability of running a business themselves. Find out why they really want you and why they can't manage alone before you commit to anything.

If you have a great idea for a business but feel the need to bring someone else in as a partner please take time to think things through carefully. It's good to have someone to share the set up costs with and any problems or challenges but as a partner they will also be entitled to half of the profits when the business becomes successful. Will their contribution be equal to yours and worthy of half the business? Are you prepared to compromise on some of your ideas and your values if they differ from your partners? Would you be better off employing someone either on a full time or part time basis therefore retaining control and keeping all of the profit?

There are many very successful partnerships but I often feel that so many of these businesses fail to reach their true potential because of the level of compromise. Often this is to safeguard a friendship or to ensure one does not tread on the toes of the other avoiding any kind of dispute.

Above all else we should be aware that partnerships are still governed in England by The Partnership Act of 1890 and unless a partnership agreement is in place partners can find themselves in bitter disputes.

If your business has high growth potential and you know that you will need to involve other people it is much better to set up a limited company with shareholders (who will take a share in the profits) and appoint Directors who will be paid a salary in relation to their role within the company and the job that they do. This allows for much more flexibility when personal circumstances change (as they tend to do over time) without things falling apart. Again make sure you have a shareholders agreement in place.

"When we first talked about starting our business we thought a partnership would be fine, keep things simple. I remembered all that you told us about partnerships and how circumstances change and realised that things were unlikely to stay the same for us. Although we both have children mine are at school and less dependent. However, I now realise that my business partner is planning to have another baby in the near future and this could leave me doing a lot more of the work to drive the business forward but still earning the same as her from the profits. If we become Ltd., as an employee she can take maternity leave and we will have more options, it won't damage the business or our relationship."

Employing People

Whether you start your business by employing staff or whether natural growth makes this a necessity, being an employer is a big responsibility. There is often a tendency to employ friends and family, people that you feel you can trust but there is a down side to this when it comes to managing them effectively, especially if performance does not meet expectations. I don't want to go too far into this subject, there's a whole new book to be written, but please keep in mind that the needs of the business must come first.

If your business is successful, organic growth will occur. Suddenly you may find that you have demands from every direction and the pressure grows. There are not enough hours in a day to get things done, it is time to expand.

Thoughts usually go towards employing someone to help with the admin and bookkeeping, this becomes an additional overhead. With an increase in overheads there is a need to bring in more revenue. Marketing needs to be stepped up and probably additional employees are needed to get through the workload. With employees comes a need to take on bigger premises to operate from. All of this can have huge cash flow implications and possibly the need to raise finance.

The reality is that most business owners are too close to their business and working so hard to keep things moving that they don't take a considered view of growing their business. Without a clear plan they often begin to bolt bits on without having a strategy to pay for it all. It's not surprising that so many businesses fail at this point. Within the growth plan it is really important to recognise the changing role of the business owner.

Most people start a business because they are good at something, and satisfaction comes from doing what they enjoy for a living. But, when the business begins to grow and other people are brought in, the business owner suddenly finds him/herself doing less and less of the part they enjoy.

There is a need to learn a new set of skills which will include being an effective manager of the business and of the people employed within it.

The inability of most business owners to delegate is another major drawback. So often they are totally unable to trust someone to do the job, assuming that no one else can do the job as well as they can. One of the problems here is this need to maintain control and to drive the business forward is what brought the business to this point of growth but it can now become detrimental in moving forward.

Key Learning Point

No one succeeds alone, choose your team carefully.

IDENTIFY YOURSELF

Naming Your Business

Starting a business is often comparable with giving birth to a baby and in the same way that we may spend hours if not weeks trying to agree a name for a new arrival the same often applies to naming a business. I remember with my first business sitting for hours with a dictionary trying to find something beginning with an 'A' so that we would be close to the beginning of the classification in the telephone directory. How things have changed.

Back in the 1980's there were many businesses with names starting with 'A' for that very same reason, the Yellow Pages telephone directory was the no. 1 advertising tool. These were in the days before the internet dominated our lives LBG (life before Google.) The emphasis then turned to having a website. Choosing the right business name is one thing but getting the right domain name for your on-line presence is essential.

"I remember our discussion about a name for my business and you suggested that I should consider using my name, because after all I am the brand. It was after you suggested this that I gave up trying to find a snazzy name and finally bought the domain name, my name."

We can get a little hung up on trying to find the right business name and in many cases it's not that important. I know of one situation where the owner of a new business was driving to the bank to open a business account, still without a business name. Knowing that he would be asked this question within the next ten minutes he looked at the road sign and named the business after the road he was driving on.

The Brand

Many people think that a brand is just a logo but it is so much more. The logo is the visual representation of the brand. Branding is about the emotion we feel when we see the logo. Think of one of your own favourite brands, Cadbury's, Kellogg's, Coca-Cola, they all conjure up feelings that we have about these companies; this impacts on our buying decisions.

What does this mean to a small business? If it's just you in your business the brand will be a reflection of you, your personality, your values and core beliefs. If you are in a partnership then it will be your shared values and beliefs.

Here is a useful exercise. Give some thought to your own core values and make a note of things that are important to you, things reflected in your personality. Mark the top three words that best sum you up. What you then have is the very essence of your brand, and this needs to somehow be captured in your brand identity, the design of your logo and possibly a strap line.

Of course if you don't have a professionally designed logo or indeed show any thought to your letterheads or business cards, this too will say a lot about you and your brand. Remember that perception is everything.

Business Cards

There are some people that can get away with cheap business cards ordered off the internet, but only a few. Your business card which carries your name and logo is one of the most important marketing tools you will use. Taking delivery of your business cards and handing the first few out is often a special moment. You really feel that you are in business.

"I remember the look on your face when I gave you one of my 'free off the internet' business cards. You told me that if I want to be taken seriously as a professional forget about the cheap business cards, invest in good branding and design from the start, it will save you money in the long term."

It's always interesting to watch people when they take your card, how they handle it, turn it over, feel the quality. Will yours stand up to this scrutiny? If someone offers me a cheaply produced business card my initial thought is that they are probably not really committed to their business. My question to them would be 'if I use your products or services, will you be there in six months time if things go wrong or if I need customer service support?' Maybe they are self-employed because of limited options and if they are offered employment they will probably take it.

There is also the other extreme where someone has invested in very expensive cards with a special finish or cut to an interesting shape. These often look great but because they are so expensive great care is taken over who they are given to, only selected potential new customers. This really misses the point of having business cards.

Key Learning Point

Your brand and your logo are a reflection of you and your values.

PROMOTING YOUR BUSINESS

If nobody knows about you and what you have to offer, it doesn't matter how good you are at what you do. It is your ability to market yourself that will determine the success of your business.

It is no good having a scatter gun approach; your marketing has to be planned and must be based on the market research you have carried out. Through your research you will know who you are targeting and you will have a profile of the typical person that you are trying to reach an understanding of their habits, their lifestyle and how to communicate with them effectively.

The next step is to develop a marketing plan. There are so many ways of promoting your business but you have to work out the best way to reach your target audience. For most businesses today it will be a combination of on-line and traditional marketing. Traditional advertising in newspapers and magazines can seem to be very expensive but your research will help you select the most cost effective place to advertise, putting you in front of your target audience. The advert needs to be designed either professionally or by you putting a great deal of thought into it. It must carry a clear, compelling message. A 'one off' advert is often a waste of money, it needs to run for a period of a few weeks or months to have any impact, if your budget restricts you to appearing only once, you may be better off saving your money.

Central to most marketing campaigns is a website, but before you have your website built you need to know how you are going to use it. Is it an on-line brochure, do you want people to buy from it, or do you just need a very simple web presence?

It is not unusual for a business to go through a period of change in the early stages of development and for this purpose I would suggest that rather than spend a lot of time and money on developing an all singing, all dancing website you should start with something quite basic. Two or three pages about the business, what you have to offer and contact details. You could spend weeks developing a site only to find that your business has taken a slightly different direction and the website no longer truly reflects what you are offering.

"I spent such a long time getting my website set up with several of pages of text and photos, it looked really good, but I was beginning to realise that my original business idea was not going to make me any money. I needed a new approach. I then realised that I needed to start from scratch with my website too, so much wasted time."

As previously mentioned it is no longer enough just to have a website. It has to be found on the World Wide Web, it needs to be fully optimised with the search engines (SEO, search engine optimisation), and this means that people can find it without typing in www . . . . Use of social media can help to bring you up higher in all search engines but being on the first page of Google is what you should aim for. Although there are other search engines Google still has 66% share at the time of writing and so this remains the measure for success.

"I decided to do a course on 'How to Build a Website', and although I learnt how to use the technical building blocks of website development I realised that I lacked the creative skills that I needed to help me design a website that looked good."

When you begin the process of identifying a web designer I strongly recommend that you choose to work with someone who offers a 'content management system'. The designer needs to include a good support package so that help is on hand to guide you in the early stages as you make changes, add photos and videos, add special offers and promotions. Stay in control. You may choose to pay someone to update your site but you need to be sure that updates will be added when you need them done, not at the convenience of others. The site must have a 'call to action' of some kind; this could be—call now, buy now, register here, download, subscribe or donate.

The great thing about websites is the ability to test and measure performance, there are many tools that you can use to find out how the website is performing, how many people have visited and which pages they have read. Learn to test and measure.

Your domain name needs to be on all of your advertising because many people having read your advertisement will check out your website before calling you. Another important point here is that they are still just as likely to telephone you rather than send an e-mail via the website. Having your landline telephone number (rather than your mobile) at the top of your website is advisable.

The next thing to think about is your marketing message to grab your potential customers' attention. It tells them why they should trust you, why they should choose to do business with you rather than your competitors, it tells them how you can solve their problem. Your message should also be a balance of features and benefits with the emphasis on benefits because people always want to know 'what's in it for me?'

"When I was trying to explain to you what my business does, I remember that at the end of every sentence you said 'and that means what to me?' It was annoying at first but eventually I was able to explain my idea in a

way in which people could understand and respond as opposed to looking slightly baffled and confused."

Try this yourself, follow each statement with 'and that means what?' by repeating this statement you should eventually be able to drill down to the core of what you have to offer and the reason why anyone would be interested in buying from you.

Once you have a clear marketing message you can use this to develop a strap line which you can include at every opportunity, on your website, business stationery, adverts etc.

Many small businesses get a great deal of success by advertising in local directories that come through your door but as with all marketing review it regularly. It may be that when you start advertising with a particular magazine it works well for you, for example, you may be the only electrician advertising and you get the lion share of the calls. But over a few weeks other electricians recognise your success and follow suit, your success rate goes down, it may be time to consider the return on your investment in that particular magazine and perhaps move your advertising elsewhere for a while.

Leaflets work well for some people although the problem is that designing and printing them is the easy part, they all have to be distributed. Many people end up with boxes of leaflets that are undelivered and out of date.

Here is the advice that Andrew Cropley of Squeaky Clean Windows shared in response to a plea for help from someone in his network.

"Many people have mixed views about leaflets and leafleting.

Leaflets do work and have worked for me, for example just today I picked up a job due to a leaflet I put though the door 2 years ago!!

My success rate has ranged from 2% to 8%. They do improve your profile and you will get work from them.

The following rules helped me:

1. *Don't pay someone to deliver them for you as they often get dumped, or distributed with others.*

2. *Ensure you deliver to every house in an area, don't assume that because one house looks rough or poor they will not use you, that may just be the 1 out of 50 which would use your service.*

3. *If when you start delivering you notice other leaflets in the letter boxes, stop and return another day. I have found that if people get lots of leaflets at once they all go in the bin.*

4. *Ensure you pay a little extra for the leaflets as you are selling a premium service. I would suggest A5 or post card. If price will run to glossy card even better, you need people to be able to pin it on to their notice boards for later!*

5. *When posting though letter boxes always put face up.*

6. *Letter boxes can be sharp so watch your fingers.*

7. *Watch out for Dogs. (Julie has 4 stitches from a dog bite while helping me one day).*

8. *Don't try to do too many hours each day (it can become soul destroying). Wear good shoes, look business like. People see you and judge you on their driveways.*

9. *If the letter box says no leaflets, don't leave one.*

10. *Always stick to the path and close gates.*

11. *Large estates are easy to deliver to because the houses are close to each other, but everyone delivers to those. I have had better result from villages because they receive less flyers.*

12. *If your car has sign writing on it ensure when leafleting that you park it in a really clear place so everyone can see it.*

13. *Mark on a map so you can see which areas you have done.*

14. *Don't discount council estates or flats as often grandparents pay the bills for their Children and Grandchildren.*

15. *The phone may not ring on the first day, but don't worry it takes time."*

Good advice. Andrew is one of a group of people who all started in business at about the same time and have become a very strong network. This group have continuously supported each other, sharing success and giving each other a boost when things have been tough.

Another way to get noticed is to write a press release for the local media. Whether it is for a newspaper, radio or T.V. the story has to be newsworthy. I run a business club for new businesses and following an excellent presentation on gaining free publicity a challenge was set to see who could get their business recognised in print. Some great stories came out.

"Seriously, I never would have either bothered or thought I had a good enough story to get into the press with it—but the competition gave me the confidence to have a go, and I am so pleased I did. It has given me a

new insight into ways of promoting what I do—plus the feedback has been really useful."

One of the most effective ways of promoting your business is through recommendation and referral. Doing a great job for your customer and having them recommend you not only gives you something to be proud of but it is certainly the cheapest way of marketing your business.

"When I first started out I tried many different ways of promoting my business but nothing has worked as well for me as referrals and recommendations. I also find that doing business with someone who has been referred is easier as they are more open and a degree of trust already exists."

For many people the product that you sell is yourself. You sell your knowledge and skills, you have to think of yourself as a product that needs to be marketed. Use of social media and having a strong on-line presence will help to achieve this and as with all other marketing a planned approach is needed to help you become an expert in your field.

"When I first started my business I signed up to every social media platform that I could, facebook, Twitter, Linked-in etc. I spent hours sending messages and communicating with my new on-line friends and followers without really knowing what I was getting out of it. I now know that I should treat it like any other form of marketing, knowing who I am targeting and getting a clear message across."

On-line marketing through a variety of social media platforms may seem like an inexpensive way of marketing your business but although the financial outlay is minimal the cost in terms of your time can be expensive. Balance your on-line presence with public speaking, radio, writing articles for local papers. It all helps to give you credibility, to become that person who is known for . . . .

Use your logo consistently on every form of marketing from your business card to the signage on your vehicle, eventually brand recognition will build.

"Keeping a marketing diary has always worked for me. Every day I write in it any form of marketing I have carried out, from attending a networking event to updating my website. If I am really busy there may be a few days when I don't manage to carry out any marketing but I know that if I want more business, this is where the effort must go in and blank pages will not bring me new business."

I have passed this marketing diary tip on to so many people, I've used it myself. It wasn't a Kate Wilde original, I first heard it mentioned at a seminar about ten years ago and others since with a little variation. One of the reasons I find it works is that we spend so much time thinking and planning what we are going to do, that we lose track of what we have put into action. By writing down what we have done rather than what we have thought about doing really helps us to recognise how much more we need to do.

There are so many ways of marketing your business, choices to be made. You just need try to find the most effective way of communicating with your target market.

You have to remember that although something has worked well in the past it may not be as effective today, keep looking out for signs of change and be ready to respond to new opportunities.

The list of options for promoting your business is endless and the more creatively you can approach this, the better.

Key Learning Point

Develop a clear compelling marketing message.

Sell, Sell, Sell

"Everyone lives by selling something"
—Robert Louis Stevenson.

So many people think that just by being really good at what they do or having a really great product it will make them successful in business, this is simply not true. You can however have a mediocre product and offer an average service and be very successful, it all depends upon your ability to get out there and sell.

For many people new to business it comes as a bit of a shock to discover that being really good at what you do is not enough. Potential customers need to know about you and what you have to offer. If the idea of having to find customers, and persuading them to buy from you has never been seriously considered then the reality of it can be a surprise.

"It's one thing being confident about your own ability in your chosen field, it's quite another to feel confident enough to sell it to others."

Many people have never considered themselves as salesmen or women but the reality is that many of us sell all the time without realising it. We persuade people to go along with our ideas, win them round to our way of thinking; we negotiate to get things on our terms or to seek a compromise. Most parents employ these skills when dealing with their children and they are totally transferable. Sales is not the dark art as some people may think.

When it comes to selling your business products or services there is no one better equipped to sell than you. Many large organisations spend thousands of pounds on sales training—teaching sales teams to overcome objections, mastering closing techniques etc. but nothing sells like enthusiasm and hopefully that is one thing you are most likely to have in abundance.

"You can't just stand back and expect a product to sell itself, you need to sell it."

The sales process is really quite a simple one and very easy to follow. People buy from people, people they have decided they like. If the person that they like is offering a product that they want (not necessarily need) and it is within their budget, there is a good chance that a sale will be made. It is my view that when you have a product or service that meets the client's needs, if it is within their budget, and you don't sell it to them, you are letting the client down. Sometimes a little persuasion to help them make a commitment is necessary.

Is it in the best interest of the client to have to continue to search until beaten down by a more successful sales person, beaten into accepting an inferior product or service to what you could have delivered? Do you really want that on your conscience?

"Something I recall you said about making your approach is the ability to step back from our business ideas to help us find a simple and compelling way to explain what we can offer to our customers."

Many years ago I worked within the financial services industry selling life assurance. This was before the Financial Services Act was introduced, and with some of the antics I witnessed this was quite possibly why it was introduced. I was paid on commission only, and after a three day induction course we were wound up to sell and sent out on the streets to do business. We had a basic knowledge of the products but immeasurable levels of enthusiasm and it was this enthusiasm that sold the products. After a few weeks we gained a little more product knowledge and were taught clever closing techniques and how to overcome objections. By then we were hungry for the next sale and that wonderful feeling of success with a clear measure of our performance in the amount of commission earned.

Selling is a numbers game and the more you practice your skills the better the ratios. I worked for this company for about 18 months and then moved away from a purely sales role but never forgot the lessons I had learnt.

What I do find surprising with many new business owners is the resistance to the concept of selling. I've worked with people that have found the idea quite distasteful and believe that if the product or service is good it will sell itself. If only this was true. So for anyone new to business but doesn't want to sell here are a few tips to consider when you meet with a prospective client:

- Always have a positive attitude.
- People buy from people, people that they like, so be nice.
- Take time to build a relationship.
- Remember to listen to what your customer is saying.
- Ask questions which will prompt a positive response.
- Plan how the meeting will conclude.
- Ask for their business.
- Be ready to discuss the financials and take their payment.

And just in case you feel uncomfortable with this just remember that if you have a great product or service that satisfies the need of the person in front of you and you don't sell it to them, you are doing them a disservice by not satisfying that need.

Key Learning Point

People buy from people they like and trust.

It's not What you know, but Who you know

To my mind the most important things in business are the relationships that you build—relationships with customers, suppliers, competitors and your peers.

Let's start by thinking about the relationship with your customers.

"Several customers have told me that they have had tradesmen in who hardly uttered a word, they come in, do the job, and are off again without any real explanation of what the problem was. I can talk for England which a lot of the older customers love. They may not know you from Adam but letting them know what the problem is (even if it goes right over their heads) gives them confidence in you."

Customer confidence is the big thing here and it should be clear to you that there is a very strong link between building confidence by taking the time to develop a relationship with your customer, and the sales process. It's all part of the same deal.

Sometimes you have to open up a bit and allow your customer to get to know you, talk about their family, your family, hobbies and interests, and discover things that you have in common. There may be things from your past experiences which you can draw on which will give them confidence in you. One thing to remember is to keep the focus on them; there is only so much they want to know about you.

I remember when I first met Trevor; he had just been made redundant from the RAF when they closed down the local base here in Norfolk. He had been an aircraft mechanic and decided to train as a plumber and to specialise in fitting bathrooms. At the time I was planning to have a new bathroom fitted and when I met him my thoughts were that working to a high standard would come naturally to him with his RAF background.

As I got to know him better I became more confident of his ability and when he fitted my new bathroom I wasn't disappointed. It took a little longer than expected but then I was one of his first customers. Some friends of mine who also had a new bathroom fitted at about that time got theirs cheaper but had complaints about the uneven tiling and other little niggles, mine was spot on.

"You told me several times to use my past experience in the RAF to gain customer confidence, and it works."

Building good relationships with your suppliers can pay dividends too. You never know when you may need a particular product or need something in a hurry to keep your customer happy and complete the job on time. If you have a good relationship with your supplier, including paying your bills on time, there is a much better chance that they will go the extra mile on your behalf.

As you continue in business you will begin to grow your own networks of people that you interact with. It has been recognised in recent years how important these networks can be to business success and you will find many different opportunities to join in. During my training sessions we spend time talking about networking and my advice is always to get out there, to get involved.

Going to a networking event can be quite scary at first so it is a good idea to practice the dreaded elevator pitch to help gain some confidence. The elevator pitch is an American expression and is based on the idea of finding yourself in a lift/elevator with someone who potentially could be your next customer. You have the time it takes for the elevator to move between floors to deliver your message and create a sales opportunity. It is really important that you are able to give a clear message about your business and what you have to offer.

One big mistake that so many people make is when someone asks 'what do you do?' they don't realise that the real question is 'what can you do for me?' So tell them what they really want to hear instead of just talking about what you do.

"I found standing up and practicing my elevator pitch in front of other people at your workshop to be terrifying but I am so glad I did it. Now when I meet people at networking events and they rattle on about themselves and what they do I think to myself—if only they had attended one of Kate's workshops I might know what they actually do by now and I smile to myself."

Having a rehearsed elevator pitch is important. It's not a speech, and if you have the opportunity to find out a little information about the person you are speaking to, you can tailor what you say to make it relevant to them. It shouldn't be a direct sales pitch (remember that the relationship comes first),it is an opportunity to give someone a clear understanding of what you do or what you have to offer and what you can do for them.

"I remember standing at the front of the workshop practicing my elevator pitch, I told you how I could prune your trees and shrubs, I could tidy your flower beds, create a beautiful lawn. In the spring I could . . . ., in the autumn . . . . You told me I was sounding quite boring, that everyone

knows what a gardener does. I know you were testing me and it seemed quite harsh but as a result of this practice session I now have an elevator pitch that I have used very effectively many time. I have also used it as an opening when meeting potential new customers with very successful results."

I've learnt over the years that networking for small businesses is very different from corporate networking which is often seen to be an opportunity to work the room and establish contacts that may be useful to you in your career. As many owners of small businesses work in isolation they see networking events as opportunities to socialise while working. This is when networking becomes more about building relationships. It's not about farming for contacts, expecting people to pass business your way after a business card exchange. Get to know them first, allow others to get to know you, to like you and to trust you, and then there is the possibility that you will do business.

Social networking overlaps with traditional networking. It can work very effectively in helping you continue to build a relationship long after the initial meeting. It can also be a way of identifying people that you would like to get to know better before you meet them. A couple of on-line exchanges gives you an easy introduction to someone ahead of a face to face meeting.

Although networking is a great way to do business it is easy to under-estimate the value of the peer support which is shared within networking groups. This can be of huge importance especially to those that have come from a large organisation background. The world of small business can be a huge culture shock especially if you have been used to having colleagues to bounce ideas around with or chat to at the coffee machine or staff canteen. There is some comfort in being with other like-minded people to share thoughts and ideas, find solutions to your problems and to share experiences.

Key Learning Point

It is the relationships that we build which hold the key to long term success in business.

CASE STUDY

Claire Wade, Founder & Director of Holidays From Home

Claire set up Holidays From Home after being bed bound and unable to travel. She creates virtual holidays and parties for people who face barriers to going out and living normally; but who still want to enjoy life. Claire brings the world to them, so they can escape reality, relax and have fun. www.holidaysfromhome.co.uk

"Setting up in business is like a rollercoaster, it's fun, exciting, scary and a real adventure. You become an expert on so many different topics, from bookkeeping to marketing, social media and PR, and that's on top of the main work you do for your business. You have to be the one to put in the hours, to get things done; but the most valuable thing I've learnt from Kate is that you need support to do that. You need people around you to encourage, cajole and sometimes push you into doing what you already know needs to be done.

Everyone running a small business benefits from being part of a group of other supportive, positive business people. Not just networking; but a specific form of peer-to-peer mentoring, where you get together at least once a month to talk about your business, where you are and what you are working to achieve. Sitting in a room with others who are going through the trials and tribulations of setting up and running a business is an incredible experience. Sharing your problems, getting advice, using your own experiences to help others and be helped in return is invaluable. You find solutions to your own and other people's problems and you come away feeling positive and supported. The businesses don't even have to be the same, they can be completely diverse, in fact the more diverse the better, because everybody brings different skill sets to the table.

Having other people to be accountable to is important, it focuses your mind and makes you get down and do the work. If you're with the right sort of people they will be there if you succeed and also if you have problems. They will listen and understand, they will want you to do the best you possibly can and you will want the same for them. It doesn't hurt to have a small sense of competition either, when you hear how well someone is doing, it can be the push you need to step up a gear and go for what you really want.

Kate has an ability to bring people together and get them talking and helping each other; but you can form your own group. Talk to people at networking meetings, find new business owners online via facebook, LinkedIn or Twitter. Start a conversation; you'll be amazed at how many people have your same fears, worries, hopes and dreams about their businesses. Owning a small business doesn't mean you have to be alone, you just have to reach out and be open. You can achieve so much more working with people, than you can by yourself."

ON THE MONEY

Funding the business

In my experience many people who are starting their first business are reluctant to take out bank loans or borrow money from any other third party. This is partly because they are playing with the unknown, the risks are high and there is uncertainty over whether the business will be a success and of course loans have to be repaid. Growing a business organically is often the preferred way forward, learning as you go, investing your savings where possible and re-investing profits back into the business.

If the business is to grow it may be necessary to consider external investment but by this time you will have gained experience and have a far greater understanding of the demands of business and the risks involved. You will have a proven track record and there will be evidence of business success which will make you a better investment proposition for any lender.

"People told me I would need at least £50,000 to start my business but I didn't want to borrow money and have such big overheads. You helped me realise that there are other ways of doing things, they may be slower but I will get to where I want to be without sleepless nights."

Building a business by the boot straps is the preferred method of many people who are just starting out but you must also make sure that the business is not underfunded; this is why cash flow forecasting is so very important.

Raising Finance

For those who have the idea, opportunity and confidence, gaining access to finance will be critical to the success of the business. If you need to approach a bank they will want to see that you understand the business cash flow, that you have developed systems for payment of suppliers and the management of poor payers. They will also want to know that the business is profitable and will want to see that actions to improve profitability have all been thought through.

A bank will also require information about the people involved in the business; this will include a profile of the business owner or management team, their investment in the business, any security available or other business interests. These help to show the strength of a business.

All businesses are different and have a variety of requirements for funding which relates to their unique needs. You may be fortunate enough to qualify for a grant to help fund starting your business. These are few and far between but that's not to say they are not available. You have to hunt them down, often they are like a best kept secret. There are websites which list all grants available nationwide; searching through them may be quite laborious but sometimes worthwhile depending upon your situation. Searching the internet for local funding is sometimes more productive and often there are little pockets of money set aside by business groups and philanthropists keen to help new businesses.

The problem with so many grants is that to qualify you need to jump through seemingly endless hoops. Consider the value of the grant and balance this against the effort required to qualify and whether you would be better off directing this energy towards developing your business.

There are other ways of raising finance, Business Angels, Venture Capitalists, and more recently there are a number of 'Micro Finance' schemes available and 'Crowd Funding'. Look these up on the internet, things change quickly and from the time of writing there are bound to be new schemes ready to be launched.

Forecasting

Having cash in the business is essential. A lack of cash is one of the most common reasons for business failure. Having funds available also enables you to take advantage of opportunities when they are presented to you. Cash is King.

Having said this often people think they need to raise finance but in reality effective cash management can keep you debt free.

It really has to be emphasised at this point just how important it is to include a cash flow forecast in your business plan, it will help you to identify peaks and troughs in your income and expenditure. A cash flow forecast will show a prediction of how much money is coming into your business against how much is going out. Any lender will almost certainly want to see a cash flow forecast included in your business plan. This is the part that many people struggle with but is very necessary. It is so much better to find out on paper if you are likely to make money from your business, or not. This is your reality check.

If your cash flow forecast does not show that you can generate sufficient income to cover the outgoing costs you need to know this at the start and do something about it. It doesn't mean you have to scrap your business idea, but you may need to think about a different approach. There are two basic things to consider, cutting costs or generating more sales. There is generally much more flexibility with income than expenditure as there is a limit to what you can cut but income can be increased through generating more sales (including up selling), increasing prices or by working longer hours.

By plotting the numbers carefully we can make sure that the money does indeed flow and that you won't run out of cash before you get off the ground.

Quite often I am told that surely a cash-flow forecast is a waste of time because although you may be able to tell what your expenditure will be, as a new business there is no way of telling how much money will come into the business. This is not strictly true. What you can do is to look at your business plan and in particular the sales and marketing elements. If you have made a full commitment to getting out and finding your customers and have a plan to make this happen, the sales that follow will be a numbers game. If your marketing amounts to little more than setting up a website and e-mailing your friends to say you are now in business then you will struggle.

"I was so glad that you encouraged me to complete my cash-flow forecast. I thought I'd worked it out in my head but on paper I soon realised that the amount of money going out was far greater than I first thought. With this information I managed to make some adjustments and I put a lot more thought into getting sales in."

Always underestimate how much and how quickly money will come in and how much more everything will cost; allow for additional expenditure.

A cash-flow forecast is usually set out on a spread sheet and it's a good idea to allow extra columns so that you can add the 'actual' figures each month. This will allow you to compare how well you are doing against what you forecast would happen and make any adjustments necessary.

Key Learning Point

Without financial management and control, your business will be like a bucket with a hole in it.

Managing Customers and Money

In a perfect world we would present our product or service, identify our customers, sell them what they need, customer is happy and pays the bill. But the world is not perfect and things don't always run so smoothly.

"You told us to always put everything in writing to our customers, even if they were mates or family. I realise now how many times I have avoided disputes with customers by doing this."

"Having been caught out by customers who found excuses not to pay up, usually for silly reasons or misunderstandings, I decided to follow your advice and get proper terms and conditions drawn up. I can see straight away how this will save me money and everyone knows where they stand, we have it in writing."

It is always a good idea to have an agreement in writing regarding the work which is to be carried out. The level of formality of the agreement will depend upon the industry and the type of work that you do. It may be that an informal e-mail to follow up a conversation will be enough. Be sure to include exactly what work is being carried out, when it is to be started and completed by, the cost and when payment is due.

The bigger the value of the work the greater the need to have a formal agreement with terms and conditions specific to your business needs. By having an agreement in writing you have something you can refer to stating exactly what has been agreed, and it will back up your case for pursuing payment should it ever become necessary to take your customer to court. A belt and braces agreement can be drawn up by a solicitor or templates downloaded and modified from various websites on the internet.

Be aware that the reality of the situation is that two people can have a conversation, reach agreement but within a very short space of time may have a totally different recollection of what was agreed. It happens, we are humans.

Credit Control

Having carried out a successful marketing campaign the enquiries flow in, the sale is made, work carried out, invoice sent, you then wait for payment. But what if the customer doesn't pay? This is where it pays to get your paperwork organised from the very beginning. If you have a contract in place or have carried out work in accordance with the specification that you provided and have completed your part of the agreement, you have every right to be paid in full. Keep a record of any telephone conversations, times, dates, who you spoke to. These together with copies of invoices, statements and letters will show evidence that you have made an effort to communicate with them and given every opportunity for payment to be made.

At this point you have to make decisions about how you want to take this forward. It may be that your customer is suffering a cash flow crisis of their own and that your patience will pay off, maybe accept part payment and set up a payment schedule.

You would be in a position to take your customer to court but there are two things to consider.

1. If you go to court the relationship with your customer will be seriously damaged so only take this route if there are no other options available to you.

2. You may not be the only creditor, there may be a long line of people that are owed money and unless you are close to the front of the queue you may just incur extra charges which may never be recovered. Secured creditors and the HM Customs & Revenue will always be at the front of the queue.

Bigger Fish

For many people there are just two different types of work, your bread and butter work which comes in regularly, it pays the bills but will never make you rich. The second type is when you get the opportunity to quote for or undertake a nice big project. Sometimes it is easy to get carried away with the situation, placing a high value on the kudos that comes with adding big firms to your customer base.

If there is a formal tender process you really need to think about how much you really want this work and weigh it up against the amount of time and effort needed to present a winning tender document. Often contracts are price driven and will go to a large contractor simply because with the economies of scale, they can deliver far more cheaply than a small business. Details must be planned to ensure that if you get the contract you have considered all costs for materials, labour and time taken to manage the project, attend meetings etc. It is so easy to miscalculate all of these if you don't take the time to work them out properly. If things are not thought through there is a good chance that you could come unstuck and under-price yourself and end up working long and hard for little return.

"Have they got a budget? Find this out before you start work on a lengthy proposal which your customer will not be able to afford."

Sometimes we can get quite excited by an invitation to submit a proposal especially if you can see that there is a lot of work to be carried out and good money to be earned. But sometimes the customer has a wonderful vision that they want you to help fulfil but no idea of the costs involved. It is only when the customer is presented with the proposal that they realise just how much money it is going to cost and there is no funding for it. By this time you will have probably put in many hours of work, all for nothing. Check if they have a budget and make sure you know who holds the purse strings.

Long Term Customer Value

You may feel you have established a good relationship with your customer, things are going well, work is progressing and they start to ask for a few extra jobs to be done 'while you're here'. It's really important that you let your customer know as you go along if there will be extra costs incurred. For example, a sweet little old lady is having a spring garden tidy up. Hedges clipped, shrubs pruned, flower beds weeded and waste disposed of. She asks about her lawn and you suggest putting some lawn feed on it, she thinks you're a nice young man and says yes please. She then finds another couple of jobs for you to do and the up-selling continues. When she is presented with the bill she is horrified at what the new total is and refuses to pay this amount. What do you do? There is a clear misunderstanding here but if you handle this situation carefully and are prepared to compromise there is a good chance you can create a win, win situation and retain a customer for the long term.

"If there is a price dispute with a customer always consider their long term value and be prepared to give a little for the greater long term gain."

Prevention is always better than a cure and so to avoid this kind of situation make sure you communicate with the customer and keep them in the picture so that the final bill is not such a shock to them. Get as much as you can in writing so that there is no uncertainty and no falling out. Even if you have carried out the agreed work and charged accordingly, if the customer feels differently your reputation can easily be damaged in the mind of the customer and anyone they choose to tell. Months of hard work spent building a solid reputation can be undone in a very short space of time.

There are times when your customer will just be trying it on, experience will teach you to recognise this and deal with it accordingly.

Key Learning Point

Ensure there is clarity when communicating with your customers and think long term.

A Matter of Confidence

For those who are determined to succeed but lack self-confidence, the secret is to pretend. Think about the way confident people talk, act, and conduct themselves, and do the same. Think of yourself as a person who is running a successful business (every day carries successes of some kind no matter how small). Learn as much as you can about everything around you, your trading environment, your competitors, your customers. Read books, study websites, and attend as many seminars, webinars, or training opportunities as you can and gradually this build up of knowledge will help you develop the confidence you need.

Confidence is one of the key ingredients of business success but that's not to say that everyone who starts a successful business feels confident. Confidence is something that develops over time, the more business success you have, the more confident you will feel. The more you learn through training to develop your craft and your business skills, the more your confidence will grow.

The secret is to fake it until you make it. No matter how much you feel you are lacking in self-confidence you must not let this show to your prospective customer. If you don't have confidence in yourself, why should they have confidence in you?

None of us are born with an abundance of self-confidence but the experiences we have in life, the skills we develop and our attitude towards achieving success are what it takes to get us there.

When I set out to write this book I asked many of the people that I have trained and advised to feed back to me any little gems of information I have shared and there was one piece of advice that stood out above the rest.

"All I need to say is 'red undies', power to the females in business."

"If I am feeling nervous about a meeting I wear red underwear for a positive feeling of power."

This may sound a little off the wall but for many people this works. If you have an important meeting to go to, perhaps with a potential new client that you really wanted to impress or a meeting with the bank manager or perhaps you have been asked to give a presentation, **wear red underwear**.

Consider this, red is the colour of energy, it is associated with movement and excitement; people surrounded by red often find their heart beating a little faster. The colour red evokes action and passion and is a perfect colour if you tend to be a procrastinator.

As red is such a powerful colour it is often not appropriate to wear a red jacket or shirt to achieve that feeling of power, it can be overpowering. But the same feeling can be achieved by wearing red underwear, and only you will know that, it's your secret and a very powerful one.

At a recent breakfast meeting I was discussing my book and whether I should try to incorporate something about red underwear in the title as an attention grabber. Later that day I received an e-mail from the person that came to give a presentation, she said "it may just be a coincidence or a subliminal message but I realised when I arrived home today that I was wearing red underwear." This was from someone who regularly speaks at international conferences and shows no fear, but sub-consciously seeks back up.

This is not just for the ladies, you men should consider getting yourselves a red thong in case of emergency; remember it's your secret.

In addition to this there are a few things that you can do to help you build confidence, for example:

Having a business plan really helps. When your ideas are laid out on a page with clear measurable goals, a strategy to help you achieve them and an understanding of how you will manage the finances and the cash flow you will feel far more in control and confident.

A professional business image enforces the feeling that you are in business. A well designed business card and letterhead, the sign writing on your vehicle all says to the world that you are in business, be proud and confident.

Get involved with networking even though it can be painful to begin with especially when you are just beginning to build contacts. It's a great feeling when you are able to walk into a room and people look up and recognise you and are able to introduce you to others. You become part of the networking scene.

Keep a success log. Get into the habit of writing down every little moment of success that you create and savour it. This could be for anything from winning a big contract, to mastering a new piece of technology, to the smile on your customers face because they are thrilled with the work you have done. Remember when you are working for yourself there is no-one to give you a pat on the back and say well done, you have to do it for yourself.

Arrogance

There is of course a very thin line that it is as well not to cross, that line is between confidence and arrogance. Arrogance is when someone displays behaviour of superiority, of always being right, over bearing in character.

These qualities do not help when building relationships with those you want to do business with. You will find that people back away from you, will avoid asking your advice and certainly will ignore any that you impose upon them. As you enjoy more and more success, remember to keep yourself in check.

Key Learning Point

Self-confident people inspire confidence in others.

CASE STUDY

Martin Wright—Wright Learn Driving School

The year 2009 was a very emotional and significant year of change for Martin Wright. As a result of redundancy he left the company he had worked at for over 23 years and just a few months later he had to deal with the sudden and unexpected loss of his Father.

These events made him think about what is important in life and how he should live it. After deciding to go travelling around the world for a few months it became apparent to Martin that he was at his happiest when helping other people to develop and learn new skills.

"When I arrived back home I started looking for a job where this 'happy feeling' could become a reality on a daily basis; this resulted in training to become a Driving Instructor. My hobbies are teaching people First Aid and how to Scuba Dive which meant I already had training skills coupled with the ability to keep calm 'under pressure'.

After a hard six months of study, exams and over 60 hours of intense 1:1 training, I qualified as an Approved Driving Instructor.

Whilst all this training was taking place I heard that business courses were available to people living in my area. So as I had never been self-employed before I thought it would be sensible to attend these.

The lady running these courses was called Kate Wilde, she was very inspirational, professional and supportive throughout each training session and provided me with lots of encouragement and ideas.

I was invited to attend monthly Mentoring Group meetings which were chaired by Kate, pulling together a wide mix of people starting a new business. This also gave me confidence and support in the early 6 months of my new business. It allowed us all to discuss any challenges we were facing and ways around them. I am grateful for the support, honesty and encouragement I received. Without this, I would not be where I am today.

It's almost been a year now since I started my driving school business and I have already gained a strong reputation for providing high quality driving lessons, tailored to each individuals need.

There have been many challenges to overcome in the early days including things like choosing a car & colour, brand name, design for the car, website, email address and business cards. I thought that all these challenges would not be that difficult but in fact they all took up a lot of my time.

I didn't want to rush into making quick decisions on any of these issues which I might later regret and so sought advice from friends and relatives. I felt it was important to get some market research done and this helped me enormously. Really though, the hardest thing to come to terms with is that ultimately everything was my final decision and no one else's.

The sense of being in control of the business is extremely satisfying but comes at a price—one which I'm happy paying!!

I'm very excited about the future for the business. After 9 months of being a Driving Instructor the business is growing month by month. Probably 95% of new clients are coming from recommendations by existing pupils, which I hope shows that I'm delivering an excellent service at the right price. This is what I enjoy the most in my job, seeing people's face the day they pass their test and knowing the time and commitment they've gone through to achieve it.

I have always been a confident person but have never run my own business, generating my own income from my own actions. Right now I feel very pleased with what I've achieved so far and hope to continue my success further by attaining more driving qualifications allowing me to teach people to become instructors themselves. I really want to be renowned for providing the best driving instruction in the area."

Keeping it in the Family

Sometimes when I ask someone new to business what their long term goals are, the answer is that they want to grow the business so that they can provide jobs for their children and to have something to pass on to them.

Although this is a nice idea it may not necessarily be what the Children want given freedom of choice. I have worked with many family businesses where the parents have brought their Children up always with an understanding that one day the business would be theirs. Often the Children have no choice in the matter; they do what is expected of them.

"I always wanted to be an architect but my Father insisted that I should come into the family business. He offered me more money than I would have received as a trainee architect and so I gave up my dream."

Sometimes things have an interesting way of working out because with the third generation of this particular family, the Father who gave up his dream encouraged his own Son to try different things. Ironically the Grandson has chosen to join the family business and has demonstrated a natural flair for it.

Having worked with many family businesses I have met a number of young men and women who never had the chance to pursue their own dreams. They had known from a young age that taking over from their parents was what was expected of them, and as dutiful children and young people this is the way things had to be. They find themselves in roles that do not necessarily match their skills and the truth is that it almost always continues to feels like the parents business even when Mum and Dad have retired, very few parents ever really let go.

Family businesses are full of complexities; they are based upon assumptions and expectations which can easily result in mistaken assumptions and unfulfilled expectations. The second generation often feel like custodians of the business, keeping it safe to pass on to their Children, making safe decisions, doing things the way their parents would have wanted.

The moral of the tale here is not to set up a business thinking that you are building something to pass on to your children, you are doing it for yourself. If your Son or Daughter naturally expresses an interest in the business, support their development by encouraging them to take a job with another firm, maybe similar to yours but in a different geographic area, or in a different industry. If they eventually join the family business they will bring so much more to their role if they have gained a wider range of experiences.

Key Learning Point

Everyone should have the opportunity to live their dream.

Summing it up

Becoming self-employed and starting a business doesn't suit everyone. There is no magic formula for success, it is the result of hard work and optimism. Sometimes luck plays a part but to quote Samuel Goldwyn "The harder I work, the luckier I get."

I have met many people over the years with great ideas for a business, it's as if they have received a gift from God, everything seems to be stacked in their favour. It's so disappointing when I send an e-mail to follow up progress and instead of an excited reply saying how busy they've been, they give me a list of reasons why things didn't go ahead, obstacles and excuses why they didn't take things forward. It's a shame when this happens but quite clearly these people are not suited to self-employment and they probably made the right decision not to go ahead.

If you do find yourself with fire in your belly and a burning desire to start a business, go for it. If writing a business plan is not for you, take time to work things out in your head, have a really good look around to get a feel for the market and your competitors, know who your customers will be and just do it.

It's a good idea to consider the worst case scenario which may not be as bad as you initially think. If you set a limit on how much you are prepared to invest, plus loss of salary from alternative employment and your time investment, how much does this really add up to? Whether you succeed or fail you will have gained a wealth of experience and knowledge, and you tried. The alternative is looking back with the regret of a lost opportunity.

If we assume that you know the job or product (the purpose of the business) inside out, the next step is to learn the necessary business skills. This includes finding customers through effective sales and marketing, keeping accounts, building and managing relationships, using and maximising the potential of information technology, complying with regulations and generating money. So many plates and you have to keep them all spinning.

It is all very exciting yet scary. The people I have worked with who have enjoyed the most success are those who are determined, to whom going back to employed work is not an option they would consider. They have usually recognised that they can't achieve all that they want to achieve on their own and have found the necessary information and support through attending workshops, sought the help of professionals, and found value in networking with other like-minded people.

If you are lucky enough to live in an area where there is a Government funded business support scheme you are at an advantage. If there is nothing available where you live it is in your interest to find some like-minded people, maybe set up your own peer support group and arrange opportunities for regular meetings. Such meetings can be at the pub, club or at the house of one of the group members. They can be informal or you can add some structure to each event and tackle a variety of issues, learning from each other.

Networking using on-line social networks helps to build relationships, share information and experiences and you can very easily join specialist or local groups with people that have common interests to your own. Join my networks, meet some of the contributors to this book on-line.

There are some pretty amazing businesses operating globally which started in a shed in someone's back garden. People that had an idea which started off quite small but as confidence grew with success, ambition kicked in. Could you be the next garden shed millionaire? Maybe success to you will mean working at something you enjoy but also having time for your family. However you define it the success of your business depends upon you making it happen and to quote Henry Ford "Whether you think you can, or you think you can't—you're right".

About the Author

'To inspire and motivate people to start, grow and succeed in business' is Kate Wilde's mission, and with this comes a real passion for helping people to make their dreams a reality.

Having gained a wealth of hands-on experience running a small business, together with academic study as a mature student, Kate felt that she was in a perfect position to support other business owners to start and grow their business.

Over the past twelve years Kate has earned a high level of credibility and respect not only with the many businesses that she has worked with but with other business professionals too. Kate has received recognition for her work through being presented with a special IBA (Institute of Business Advisers) award for 'Innovative use of Advisory Skills' in 2006 and in 2008 she was awarded 'Best Business Supporter' by Enterprising Women. In 2011 she was appointed as one of 50 enterprising women in the UK who are working alongside women and girls to encourage them to consider starting and growing businesses.

Based close to the beautiful Norfolk Broads and surrounded by 70 miles of coastline Kate lives with her partner Mike Barker who she met when he attended one of her workshops. Mike successfully runs his own garden and landscape business. She also has a grown-up daughter, Verity.

Glossary of Business Terms

BACS
Bankers' Automated Clearing Services is a United Kingdom scheme for the electronic processing of financial transactions.

Balance Sheet
A Statement which shows the assets and the liabilities of a company on a particular date.

Brand
A name, design or symbol which gives an identity to a company, a product or service.

Business Angel
Private individual who is looking to invest in companies likely to achieve high growth.

Cash flow
The movement of money in and out of a business.

Copyright
A concept which gives the creator of an original piece of work exclusive rights to it.

Demographics
The study of populations in relation to size, density and age.

Entrepreneur
Someone who undertakes an enterprise, owns and manages a business.

Gross Profit
The amount of money brought into a company minus the direct cost of those sales.

Intellectual Property (IP)
Property such as copyright, trademarks and patents, which have no tangible form but representing the product of creative work or invention.

Market Research
Research to determine consumers' opinions about a product or service.

Marketing
The process that identifies, anticipates and supplies customer requirements efficiently and profitably.

Mentor
A trusted adviser.

Mission Statement
A statement of the business aims of an organisation.

Net Profit
The measure of profitability of a company after taking into account all costs incurred.

Niche market
Addressing a need for a product or service that is not being addressed by mainstream providers.

Overheads
The operating costs of running a business including rent, salaries, printing, advertising and depreciation etc.

Patent
An official document conferring sole rights for a term of years to the proceeds of an invention.

Profit and Loss Account
An account showing income and expenditure into a business usually balanced annually to show the amount of profit or loss.

Target Customers
The identification of a group of specific customers to help you deliver a clear marketing message.

Trademark
A symbol, sound, word or words legally registered or established by use as representing a company or product.

Turnover
The monetary value of total sales over a period.

USP
Unique selling point.

Venture Capital
Money provided by individual investors or business organisation for new speculative enterprises.

INDEX

Join 'The Wilde World' for Free

Visit www.engagewithbusiness.co.uk and sign up for a newsletter for on-going information and support to help keep your business momentum going.

Join us on facebook http://www.facebook.com/TheWildeWorld

Join us on YouTube http://www.youtube.com/TheWildeWorld

Join us on Twitter @TheWildeWorld